Ask Him

JANE TRUFANT HARVEY

Ask Him

Simple Words to Jumpstart Your
Conversation with God

WELLSPRING
North Palm Beach, Florida

wellspring

Design by Ashley Wirfel

ISBN: 978-1-63582-157-4 (hardcover)
ISBN: 978-1-63582-158-1 (e-Book)

10   9   8   7   6   5   4   3   2   1

Printed in the United States of America

When Words Fail You

I AM SO EXCITED FOR YOU. The book you have in your hands will change your life. If you let it. How can I be so sure? It changed my life—and I have recommended it to so many other people who have also had their lives transformed by it.

But first, let me provide some context and backstory.

My father died of cancer when I was thirty, and eighteen months later, my eldest brother Mark was killed in a car accident. When my father died, I was sad, but he had lived an amazing life. When my brother died, I felt like he had been ripped from a life half-lived. His daughters were too young to lose their father, his brothers were too young to lose their eldest brother. And the compounding effect of losing them both in such a short period of time knocked me off balance. The sadness sunk in, and some days it just seemed to get deeper and deeper.

At my annual physical with my doctor he asked me how I was doing, and I told him I was struggling. He suggested I see a therapist. Like millions of people, I had a stigma against therapy. Australia isn't exactly a haven of therapeutic embrace. Most Australian's idea of therapy is, "Have another beer mate and everything will be fine." Nonetheless, I overcame the stigma and went to see the therapist my doctor had suggested.

It was good for me. It was healthy just to talk through some things with someone who had no agenda for my life. One of the most profound and practical things the therapist said to me was, "When words fail you, let them." I am a wordsmith by trade, so it doesn't seem right to let words fail me. I have spent so much of my life looking for the right words. Failing to find the right words didn't sit well with me, so this was a particularly difficult lesson for me. But over time as I observed myself and others, I realize how profound her advice was.

Over the years, I have realized that there are no words for some situations. It wouldn't matter if you were Shakespeare or Wordsworth, Shelley or Byron, there are simply no words to comfort a mother who has lost her child. This is just one of many situations that leave us speechless for a reason. They leave us speechless because these moments are not the right time or place for words. In these moments all we can do is be with each other or give grief its space. All we can do is honor the wishes of the one who is suffering and be with them or not (according to their need and preference).

The other situation where words fail me more often than I would like is in prayer. Here, I have learned many lessons. Sometimes when words fail us in prayer it is because God simply wants us to be still and quiet and be with him. At other times, when words fail us in prayer it can be because we are anxious, busy, and distracted with the things of this world. At these times it can help to use someone else's words. I have heard of writers experiencing writer's block who would use the opening lines or paragraphs of another writer's work to get them started. Other people's prayers can be very powerful in getting our own conversation started with God also.

For years when words failed me in prayer, I turned to Psalm 23. It never let me down. I can pray it over and over again, it never gets old, never loses its meaning, often brings me to tears, and always restores my faith, hope, courage, and love.

Psalm 23
The Lord is my shepherd, there is nothing I shall want;
he lets me lie down in green pastures.
He leads me beside still waters;
he restores my soul.
He leads me in paths of righteousness for his name's sake.
Even though I walk through the valley of the shadow of death,
I will not be afraid; for the Lord is at my side;

his rod and his staff, they comfort and protect me.
He prepares a table for me in the presence of my enemies;
He anoints my head with oil, my cup overflows.
Surely goodness and mercy shall follow me all the days of my life; and
I will live in the house of the Lord forever.

During one of the most difficult times in my life I discovered Jane Trufant Harvey and this book, *Ask Him*. It has never been far from me since.

One of the most difficult things in this life is to learn how to speak to God as a friend. There is genius in these pages, because with each page, Jane prompts us to have a conversation with God.

Who is guiding your life? How is that working out for you? Is it time for a change? Are you ready to allow God to guide you in all things? Ask Him!

Allow God to surprise you, to sweep you away, to show you what it means to be deliriously happy, to teach you to dance for joy. Until we do, I am not sure we have really lived at all. To live this life and not to explore the spiritual life deeply would be a tragedy.

Ask Him!

- MATTHEW KELLY

I.

Ask Him...

to surround you with
His protection and peace.

2.

Ask Him...

to remind you when
you are feeling unworthy,
that you are perfect in His eyes.

3.

Ask Him...

to bless your eyes so that
you see the goodness in people,
especially when it is so easy to find fault.

4.

Ask Him...

to forgive you when
your humanness overrides your faith.

5.

Ask Him...

to let the Holy Spirit inspire
a sense of peace, joy, and hope that
is reflected in everything you do.

6.

Ask Him...

to help you remember that feeling
cherished is something you not only
deserve but what He desires for you.

7.

Ask Him...

to bring restoration to your broken
relationships, according to His will.

8.

Ask Him...

to remind you that prayer
will sustain you through the
most difficult times in your life.

9.

Ask Him...

to constantly remind you that life is *not* about what you have.

10.

Ask Him...

to constantly remind you that life
is about who you are and your
commitment to make the world
a better place because you are here.

11.

Ask Him...

to give you freedom from fear,
freedom to trust, freedom to endure,
and freedom to forgive.

12.
Ask Him...

for patience when you want answers.

13.

Ask Him...

to bless you abundantly with the
richness of good, Godly people who
will challenge you to be the person
He Created you to be.

14.

Ask Him...

to help you to remember that
the most important thing in life
is to *love* and be loved.

15.

Ask Him...

to teach you how to be happy
when someone else wins.

16.

Ask Him...

to help you discern the difference
between a need and a desire.

17.

Ask Him...

to give you the courage to bravely reveal that you have weaknesses and fears; and when you fall down or make mistakes, to give you the strength to take responsibility for them.

18.

Ask Him...

to remind you to pray for your country, for other countries, and the people within them who are oppressed.

19.

Ask Him…

to help you to remember not to be anxious about *anything*, that God promises He will guard your heart and mind with peace.

20.

Ask Him...

to remind you that random acts
of kindness are contagious.

21.

Ask Him...

to help you laugh more—and more often.

22.

Ask Him...

for His awesome presence when you speak words of encouragement to a wounded spirit.

23.

Ask Him...

to help you truly *know* in your soul that
you are worthy, capable, smart, beautiful,
and good enough just because you *are* . . .
because God's promises will be so
infused in your soul that these things
become *truth* for you, not just
what you *wish* the truth to be.

24.

Ask Him...

to restrain your tongue when you are
responding to someone who has hurt you.

25.

Ask Him...

to help you remember that
excellence is *not* perfection.

26.

Ask Him...

to bring you to a place of stillness
and solitude so that you can hear
His voice—even if He is whispering.

27.

Ask Him...

to allow your mouth to utter words
of gentle kindness—words that exhibit
respect and words that inspire
compassion.

28.

Ask Him...

to give you an awareness that when
you feel as though something is missing . . .
it's usually Him.

29.

Ask Him...

to remind you that you have the ability
to change lives . . . with a smile.

30.

Ask Him...

to help you believe that you were chosen,
hand-picked by God, to do His will;
that with Him, you can accomplish
miraculous things.

31.

Ask Him...

to help you be of a generous spirit to everyone, not just to those who aren't as fortunate as you are. Sometimes "fortunate" people are needy, too.

32.

Ask Him...

to remind you that *hope* is that little ray of light in the middle of the terrifying darkness.

33.

Ask Him...

to renew your heart so that
when people see you,
they *know* God dwells within you.

34.

Ask Him...

to help you to be quick to ask for
forgiveness, and to realize that
real peace often requires the grace
to forgive yourself.

35.

Ask Him...

to instill perseverance when you are tired.

36.

Ask Him...

to empower you to trust Him, even
through tragic and trying circumstances.

37.

Ask Him...

to give you the strength to surprise your friends and children with kindness and comforting words when they make mistakes, instead of disappointment or anger.

38.

Ask Him...

to continue to uncover the
amazing grace that emerges when you
have a humble heart.

39.

Ask Him...

to remind you to choose *truth*.

40.

Ask Him...

to show you how to love people
in a way that they are *unmistakably*
sure that it is pure and authentic.

41.

Ask Him...

to remind you that you are only
limited when you lack *faith*.

42.

Ask Him...

to help you resist the temptation
to listen in silence as someone's
name is unjustly being tarnished.

43.

Ask Him...

to open your heart to allow you to discover, develop, and use the specific spiritual gifts He has chosen for you in an unselfish way and for His glory.

44.

Ask Him...

to help you to *rest* in His sufficiency.

45.

Ask Him...

to give you a spirit of complete
surrender so that He can do
His will—His plan through you.

46.

Ask Him...

for clarity when you are feeling *overwhelming* confusion.

47.

Ask Him...

to teach you how to accept
disappointments with grace and character.

48.

Ask Him...

to give you the courage to speak out
when you see injustice.

49.

Ask Him...

to remind you when you begin to think
your mistakes are bigger than everyone
else's that He'll whisper, "Did you forget . . .
whoever makes the most mistakes wins!"
. . . and you laugh with relief.

50.

Ask Him...

to give you a thirst for His word
so it will infuse your life with its
wisdom, courage, and hope.

51.

Ask Him...

to help you to be more tolerant.

52.

Ask Him...

to give you the *wisdom*,
but more importantly,
the *fortitude* to walk in His way.

53.

Ask Him...

to help you comprehend the magnitude
of the words: The greater the sin,
the greater the sinner has the right
to His healing mercy.

54.

Ask Him...

to instill in you a strong sense of
community, and to remind you that
He created other people so that you
wouldn't have to handle things alone.

55.

Ask Him...

to reassure you that when you are
at your weakest, *He* is at His strongest.

56.

Ask Him...

to remind you fear does not come from Him, so don't allow your life to be controlled by fear.

57.

Ask Him...

to remind you that being obedient when you lack understanding is taking a leap in faith that will never go unnoticed.

58.

Ask Him...

to never let you forget: *Life* is not about competition, it is about striving to reach another level of achievement in being a better *you*.

59.

Ask Him...

to give you the courage to step
outside yourself, and *closer* to Him.

60.

Ask Him...

to help you recognize the need for Him every single day—not just when there is trouble.

61.

Ask Him...

to discourage you from focusing
on the times that you fail: to focus instead
on the abounding hope into
which He has called you.

62.

Ask Him...

to help you willfully accept that death *does not* mean the end for you or someone you love; it is only a temporary separation you are called to endure until you are reunited in eternity.

63.

Ask Him...

for the awareness that when you are *extremely angry*, it usually means that you were *extremely hurt* first.

64.

Ask Him...

to help you understand that life
can't always be happy and fun . . .
sometimes you learn the most when your
life is *temporarily* a total disaster.

65.

Ask Him...

to help you appreciate the reality that
love is an *action* word.

66.

Ask Him...

to help you see that doing the very *least* you can to get by will undermine what you are *truly* capable of doing.

67.

Ask Him...

to break the chains of *emotional bondage* that have kept you from experiencing the *true peace* He desires for you.

68.

Ask Him...

to remind you that though there will be times your best efforts don't get recognized by those around you—He never misses a thing.

69.

Ask Him...

to gently remind you that *sometimes* His timing won't coincide with your *schedule*.

70.

Ask Him...

to help you rejoice when you feel empty, since He can't pour His spirit into something that is already full.

71.

Ask Him...

to lovingly develop you spiritually
so that He may use you as
His example for others.

72.

Ask Him...

to remind you that *sometimes* people say things that they wish, with all their heart, they could take back.

73.

Ask Him...

to bless you with the conviction that being a faithful friend is the most extraordinary gift you can give to another person.

74.

Ask Him...

to help keep you from judging the
motivation of someone else's heart.

75.

Ask Him...

to sustain you while you are away—
so you can return with *honor*.

76.

Ask Him...

to discourage you from withholding affection from the people you love, as an expression of disapproval.

77.

Ask Him...

to remind you that being critical of
someone insinuates—not only to them,
but to others—that they are
somehow inadequate.

78.

Ask Him...

to remind you that when someone is speaking to you and you stop what you are doing, look directly at them and really listen, you affirm that they are valuable.

79.

Ask Him...

to reassure you that when you are
saying, "I can't." He is saying,
"Yes you can . . . need some help?"

80.

Ask Him...

to help you let go of any *bitterness*
that is poisoning you.

81.

Ask Him...

to help you remember that striving for perfection often results in intolerance.

82.

Ask Him...

to give you the freedom to easily say "NO," because you have discovered a deeper "YES!"

83.

Ask Him...

to give you the grace to do what is *right*,
even when you are *alone*.

84.

Ask Him...

to inspire a change in *you* every time you have thoughts of changing someone else.

85.

Ask Him...

to reassure you that when you are feeling
unlovable, He will always love you.

86.

Ask Him...

to help you stand strong in the battle
between your divine spirit,
which encourages you to choose
excellence, and your humanness,
which finds satisfaction in mediocrity.

87.

Ask Him...

to help you remember that with every decision you make and every action you take, you're being an example to someone else—*good and bad.*

88.

Ask Him...

for compassion, strength, and courage to
keep loving someone *in* their addiction.

89.

Ask Him...

to show you how to look for the lesson when something goes wrong, instead of looking for someone to blame.

90.

Ask Him...

to remind you that He
doesn't ask you to be successful ...
He only asks you to be faithful.

91.

Ask Him...

to watch you soar as you discover that
He designed you for GREATNESS.

92.

Ask Him...

to reassure you as you learn to trust Him
with your life, and that there is comfort
even in discomfort.

93.

Ask Him...

to help you remember that the *mercy*
He shows you today, means you can stop
being stressed about yesterday.

94.

Ask Him...

to manifest His strength in
you—when you are overcome
by feelings of powerlessness.

95.

Ask Him...

to assure you that He's already equipped you with everything you need *before* He calls you to step forward for Him.

96.

Ask Him...

for the strength to give your *best* when
someone else is at their worst.

97.

Ask Him...

to help you remember that He wants
you to *learn* from your past,
not wallow in it.

98.

Ask Him...

to help you prayerfully make a list
of what's MOST important in life—
and the wisdom to refer to it when
you've lost perspective.

99.

Ask Him...

to give you the *willingness* to compromise when you find yourself at an impasse with someone you love.

100.

Ask Him...

to remind you that through His grace,
you can FINALLY forgive that
person you've never been able to
fully forgive before.

101.

Ask Him...

for patience when your day starts out bad
and ends up worse ... and to remind you
that He affectionately calls this
"Character Building 101."

102.

Ask Him...

to keep you from being misled by the type of joy that is temporary, superficial, and deceiving. Authentic joy is being right with God.

103.

Ask Him…

to give you the grace to believe, when you find yourself struggling with unbelief.

104.

Ask Him...

for the humbled realization when you are
feeling completely self-sufficient,
that you woke up this morning because
HE wanted you to.

105.

Ask Him...

to help you remember that in order to
encounter the Holy Spirit you must first
surrender to the Holy Spirit.

106.

Ask Him...

for an uncompromising sense of fairness
in the face of conflict.

107.

Ask Him...

to sustain you when your problems have you dejected and discouraged, and to help you remember they're only temporary, not permanent.

108.

Ask Him...

to remind you that as a human being,
you often view your life from a human
perspective, with human limitations, when
in fact, you have a God with unlimited
power ready to transform your life into
something more than you could ever
dream or imagine.

109.

Ask Him...

to help you resist being so proud that you miss the opportunity to be vulnerable with someone you can share your inner most struggles with.

110.

Ask Him...

to take away your desire to want more
than the will of God.

III.

Ask Him…

when you are feeling like you can never do or be enough, that you are perfectly and completely enough for Him.

112.

Ask Him...

to instill in you that unshakable peace
comes from unwavering faith.

113.

Ask Him...

to encourage you to offer up all
the heartache and suffering you're
called to endure for the healing
and intentions of others.

114.

Ask Him...

for restored optimism when
you're feeling discouraged.

115.

Ask Him...

to quietly carry away any arrogance and self-importance you're unconsciously flaunting in front of others.

116.

Ask Him...

to remind you of the awesome privilege it is to be the only thing He created that can address Him in prayer.

117.

Ask Him...

to help you see that although choices
are what brought you where you are
today, choices can also bring you
a different tomorrow.

118.

Ask Him...

for more teachable moments.

119.

Ask Him...

for obstacles, not impasses.

120.

Ask Him...

to help you see constructive criticism
as a valuable tool in developing
humility and virtue.

121.

Ask Him...

to remind you that often times when you're busy rebelling, He's desperately trying to protect you from yourself.

122.

Ask Him...

to rescue you from drowning
in self-doubt.

123.

Ask Him...

to give you the strength to follow Him when the popular crowd is heading in the opposite direction.

124.

Ask Him...

to go before you always,
in everything you do.

125.

Ask Him...

to not let you slip into a routine
of taking the gift of each new day for
grated; to be mindful that they're
a personal gift from Him.

126.

Ask Him...

to remind you that your gift to Him,
is how you choose to use each day
that He's entrusted to you.

127.

Ask Him...

to help you take advantage of
every opportunity to reach out to
the lonely and discouraged.

128.

Ask Him…

in the midst of hardships
to notice you seeking His grace,
not questioning your faith.

129.

Ask Him...

to help you come to the end of yourself
so you can start living wholly through Him.

130.

Ask Him...

to remind you that HE WILL NEVER give
up on you, even when you find it so easy
to give up on yourself.

131.

Ask Him...

to help you live each day
with passion and purpose.

132.

Ask Him...

to help you understand that riches are in
relationships not in possessions.

133.

Ask Him...

if today is your last day on earth;
that your thoughts, words and actions
would be pleasing to Him.

134.

Ask Him...

to remind you that it is not always
your words—but the tone of them—
that can wound the soul.

135.

Ask Him...

to help you recognize that
sometimes you are too close to
a situation to think rationally.

136.

Ask Him...

to remind you that He gets
enormous pleasure showering
His grace on humble hearts.

137.

Ask Him...

to abundantly bless the people who have been an encouragement to you.

138.

Ask Him...

for His mercy to wash over you
when you've disappointed Him ...
and yourself.

139.

Ask Him...

when you find yourself hiding behind the fear of being judged and the desire for acceptance from others, to give you His supernatural courage to see the beauty and splendor in your authentic self.

140.

Ask Him...

to show you what it takes to thrive,
not just survive.

141.

Ask Him...

to help you remember how incredibly
important it is to do what you
say you'll do.

142.

Ask Him...

when you're feeling defeated, to give you inspiration to emerge with a renewed sense of purpose.

143.

Ask Him...

to take away your resistance to change . . .
and replace it with the thrill of possibility.

144.

Ask Him...

to transform you into a fearless seeker
of truth, liberty, and justice.

145.

Ask Him...

to help you find relief in
His arms of mercy.

146.

Ask Him...

to help you let go of any "friend"
that isn't supporting and helping you
to be the best you can be.

147.

Ask Him...

to remind you that it is *never* too late
to change a decision that will result
in the greater good.

148.

Ask Him...

to be your biggest advocator and encourager when you genuinely act with the most honorable intentions; but still somehow manage to create a monumental disaster.

149.

Ask Him...

to remind you that in order to really get to know the promptings of God, you must be willing to spend some time in the classroom of silence.

150.

Ask Him...

if he would be so kind as to give you just
a little hint of His ultimate goal
when you feel like He's testing you
beyond your limits.

151.

Ask Him...

if you are accepting the proper
responsibility for your part of an
argument.

152.

Ask Him...

to lift you in your brokenness
and gently carry you to the safety
of His unconditional and redeeming love.

153.

Ask Him...

to please knock a little louder on the door of your heart if for some reason you've missed His call before.

154.

Ask Him...

for courage and self-assurance when you
stand up for and speak the truth to a
world that doesn't necessarily want
to hear the truth.

155.

Ask Him...

for an added supply of self-control when your confronted with things you *really* WANT . . . but don't *really* need.

156.

Ask Him...

to remind you that more
is not necessarily better!

157.

Ask Him...

to remind you if you're lost,
the way of the cross leads home.

158.

Ask Him...

to keep you from meddling in the
problems He's handling for you today.

159.

Ask Him...

to remind you that, contrary to popular belief, you don't have to have all the answers!

160.

Ask Him...

to remind you that you are not called,
nor required, to impress your fellow man.

161.

Ask Him...

to persuade you to step outside your circumstances and look to Him for guidance.

162.

Ask Him...

to encourage you to dream big!

163.

Ask Him...

to somehow, someway, somewhere,
reveal himself to you every day.

164.

Ask Him...

to help you start today with a good attitude—and even more gratitude.

165.

Ask Him...

to remind you that He'll just listen
to your heart when you're finding it
difficult to pray.

166.

Ask Him...

to remind you that He will meet you in the good, the bad, and the ugly of exactly where you are today.

167.

Ask Him...

to remind you that there are no accidents,
no conditions, and no setbacks that are
greater than God.

168.

Ask Him...

to help you accept that you cannot
have a different yesterday, but you CAN
influence a different today.

169.

Ask Him...

to remind you that failure is an event,
not a person.

170.

Ask Him...

to pour out His protection and abundant blessings to the men and women who fight for your freedom.

171.

Ask Him...

to remind you if you want respect,
conduct yourself in a manner worthy
of respect.

172.

Ask Him...

to give you the grace to identify things
that contributes to a spirit of
self-centeredness . . . and the humility to
welcome change.

173.

Ask Him...

to remind you that the best way
to find yourself, is to give yourself.

174.

Ask Him...

to remind you that when you pray with limitations, you're denying Him a chance to do miraculous things.

175.

Ask Him...

to give you the capacity to adapt to unexpected circumstances, instead of getting distressed and anxious.

176.

Ask Him...

if idolizing means excessively loving
something or someone more than Him.
Who or what in your life
is distracting you?

177.

Ask Him...

to remind you that your strength of patience is frequently acquired through the endurance of trials.

178.

Ask Him...

to remind you that resourceful people always have a plan "B"!

179.

Ask Him...

to remind you that idolatry is worshipping created things in place of the creator.

180.

Ask Him...

to remind you that doing an act
of kindness in the spirit of Christ
purifies the motive.

181.

Ask Him...

to help you remember that to some
He's just another one, but to us,
He's the only one.

182.

Ask Him...

to remind you of the sense of peace
and comfort that comes from knowing
you're in the hands of Christ.

183.

Ask Him...

if He would mind if you carved out some time during your day to just wallow in the majesty of being a child of the king?

184.

Ask Him...

to place His grace between
you and your shame.

185.

Ask Him...

to release you from whatever
keeps you separated from Him

186.

Ask Him...

when you are lost and in need
that He alone is whom you seek.

187.

Ask Him...

to tell you again that through Him you are
worthy and cherished and magnificent.

188.

Ask Him...

to remind you that He began a good work in you, and He will complete it.

189.

Ask Him...

to be the treasure that you seek.

190.

Ask Him...

not to let anything that is troubling you,
overshadow the love He has for you.

191.

Ask Him...

to help you breathe in the fragrance
of His peace and exhale the anxiety
that keeps you stressed.

192.

Ask Him...

to help you remember to tell your children that they are a blessing, that they have a purpose, and that they bring value to this life.

193.

Ask Him...

to remind you that no matter
what life throws at you, together,
He'll help you through it.

194.

Ask Him...

to help you remember when your
children hear you wounding each other
when you argue, they feel distressed
and helpless.

195.

Ask Him...

to come amid the suffering
in your body and restore you.

196.

Ask Him...

to be strong within you when
the enemy wants to keep you down
and helpless.

197.

Ask Him...

to keep you vigilant in prayer
when our nation's in crisis.

198.

Ask Him...

to help you see a future filled with
promise and potential.

199.

Ask Him...

in the ache of loneliness to send
a tender heart to comfort you.

200.

Ask Him...

to give you the wisdom to know
how to nurture your spouse's spirit
when it's deflated.

201.

Ask Him...

to remind you that He wants your
future to be bigger than your past.

202.

Ask Him...

to help you make it a priority
to spend carefree timelessness
with the people you love.

203.

Ask Him...

to remind you that sustaining joy is achieved by sustaining others.

204.

Ask Him...

to teach you that self-discipline is
a bridge to freedom.

205.

Ask Him...

to develop in you a spirit of generosity and goodwill when you find yourself engaging with people who have a different opinion than yours.

206.

Ask Him...

to teach you how to confront
with compassion.

207.

Ask Him...

to remind you how important it is to tell people how they've impacted your life before they die . . . instead of at their eulogy.

208.

Ask Him...

to help you remember that the difference
between pleasure and happiness is that
pleasure cannot be sustained beyond the
experience that created the pleasure.

209.

Ask Him...

to give you the ability to identify your weaknesses and transform them into strengths.

210.

Ask Him...

to remind you that it is a common misconception that you will find happiness without sacrifice.

211.

Ask Him...

to remind you that there is something extremely powerful when people get together in the mutual pursuit of dreams.

212.

Ask Him...

to remind you that great leaders
emerge arguing FOR something not
against something.

213.

Ask Him...

to remind you that love is not based on understanding but acceptance.

214.

Ask Him...

to remind you to consult with Him when you're working on a project. He has an uncanny way of thinking outside the box.

215.

Ask Him...

to remind you that the grass
IS greener on His side.

216.

Ask Him...

to help you recognize that time after time,
truth is revealed in adversity.

217.

Ask Him...

to help you hunger for time
alone in His presence.

218.

Ask Him...

to help you to know the soothing sound
of His heartbeat ... because you've
drawn close enough to hear it.

219.

Ask Him...

to remind you that He speaks to you through other people; don't let their outside appearance keep you from missing His message.

220.

Ask Him...

when you're feeling rejected
to remind you that He chose you
before the foundation of the world.

221.

Ask Him...

to find you if you're lost.

222.

Ask Him...

to remind you that your children
need to see you engage in life's
challenges not cower from them.

223.

Ask Him...

to give you the grace to trust Him *and* His timing when you're feeling anxious about the spiritual welfare of your children.

224.

Ask Him...

to give you an opportunity to personally experience how a clear conscious not only liberates but brings peace and harmony to the heart.

225.

Ask Him...

to remind you that His commitment never changes . . . He will not leave you . . . He will not fail you . . . He will not forsake you.

226.

Ask Him...

for the grace to not only walk in
His spirit but to walk obediently.

227.

Ask Him...

if He can come to work with you today.

228.

Ask Him...

to help you stop projecting what you
THINK someone else is thinking.

229.

Ask Him...

to give you the inner strength to cope with rejection so you'll confidently refuse to let it wound your spirit.

230.

Ask Him...

to give you a tender heart to love people
who are extremely difficult to love.

231.

Ask Him...

to intervene when you are about to hurt
the people you love the most.

232.

Ask Him...

to remind you that we are not perfect . . .
just perfectly forgiven.

233.

Ask Him...

to remind you that His arms
never get weary helping you back
to your feet when you fall.

234.

Ask Him...

to remind you that He wants *you*
to be one of the saints when they
go marching in.

235.

Ask Him...

to remind you when you see a magnificent sunset that He did that for you!

236.

Ask Him...

to help you achieve the goal of
making the length of time that you fall
from His grace and the time you ask for
His mercy shorter and shorter.

237.

Ask Him...

to remind you when you are far away,
He is near; and when you are near,
He is content.

238.

Ask Him...

to help you let go when He's pulling you in a different direction than *you* think is best.

239.

Ask Him...

if it is in keeping with His perfect plan for you, that He reveal any illness in your body so your health may be completely restored for His glory.

240.

Ask Him...

to help you pray for, instead of judge people, whose behavior is atrocious.

241.

Ask Him...

to help you quit the negative and destructive inner dialogue that is keeping you from realizing your dreams.

242.

Ask Him...

to challenge you to live your life ...
like you were dying.

243.

Ask Him...

to help you be successful in discovering the different ways each one in your family needs to be loved.

244.

Ask Him...

to help you graciously and gratefully
accept a compliment.

245.

Ask Him...

to help you not be consumed by the materialism of holiday craziness.

246.

Ask Him...

to remind you that unforgiveness
is like drinking poison and thinking
the other person will die.

247.

Ask Him...

to remind you that the influence
YOU have on other people is substantially
more than you can imagine.

248.

Ask Him...

to help you remember to use things
and love people, not love things
and use people.

249.

Ask Him...

to remind you to pray for your enemies.

250.

Ask Him...

if He'd pick someone out for you
today so you can do a random
act of kindness for them.

251.

Ask Him...

to help you want to serve instead
of wanting to be served.

252.

Ask Him...

to distract your mind when you
find yourself wanting to masterfully
manipulate a situation.

253.

Ask Him...

to encourage you to speak words of life,
words of respect, and words of
forgiveness to and over your family.

254.

Ask Him...

to remind you that for ALL of your life,
He will continuously, without ceasing,
pursue your heart.

255.

Ask Him...

to remind you that He doesn't
just give peace, He is peace.

256.

Ask Him...

to help you recognize if you've gotten
so comfortable pretending your life is
fine that you can't hear your spirit crying
out for something more.

257.

Ask Him...

to remind you that what's seen is only temporary, but what's unseen is eternal.

258.

Ask Him...

to help you remember that the
authentic joy found in Christ
is radically different than the
hypocritical joy found in the world.

259.

Ask Him...

for His word to richly dwell
in your inner most being.

260.

Ask Him...

to help you master the discipline
of simply living one day at a time.

261.

Ask Him...

to remind you that a Spirit-filled heart intentionally lines up to care for the well-being of others.

262.

Ask Him...

to remind you that sometimes
He doesn't want to use someone else
for His vision and plan ... He wants YOU,
no matter how much you try to
convince Him otherwise.

263.

Ask Him...

to remind you that like a warm blanket when you're cold, is His presence when you're feeling alone.

264.

Ask Him...

if He would help keep your self-defeating fears in check so you don't sabotage the wonderful things that are coming your way.

265.

Ask Him...

to remind you that ignorance of Sacred
Scripture is ignorance of Him.

266.

Ask Him...

to remind you that in order to really
know someone, you must spend time with
them ... God is no different.

267.

Ask Him...

to remind you to just do the next right
thing when you make mistakes.

268.

Ask Him...

to help you remember not to focus on the road ahead, just take ONE step toward Jesus. Have the courage to surrender that one step for Him today.

269.

Ask Him…

to remind you that He wants the best for you, and joy and happiness are part of His best for you!

270.

Ask Him...

to remind you that when everything is over, it's your faith, not your fortune that will bring Him praise, honor, and glory.

JANE TRUFANT HARVEY is the author of the popular gift book series: *Ask Him for Encouragement, Ask Him for Hope, Thank Him, Saints Alive,* and *Ask Him for Courage with Cancer.*

Visit AskHimBooks.com

Jane is an avid reader, an enthusiastic golfer, and an indefatigable community volunteer. She cherishes time with her family. She and her husband Bobby have been married for 42 years and are the proud parents of four children, Elizabeth, Lauren, Bobby, III, and Taylor. They have five precious grandchildren: Cade Nicholas, Austin Joseph, Emily Joyce, Olivia Jane, and Robert Gerard, IV. You can email Jane at info@askhimbooks.com.